Success from the Ashes:
How to Triumph after Failure

Richard P Swanson

Founder of Learning Meets Quality LLC

ISBN-13: 978-1500546878

ISBN-10: 1500546879

About Richard P Swanson

Learning Meets Quality founder Richard P Swanson is a career chemist, educator, and project manager who has worked in the education, non-profit, and for-profit arenas. He has led projects in such diverse areas as health and safety, media production, chemical manufacturing, and small business development. Rick holds degrees in chemistry, education, and the history of science and technology, and is trained as a Six Sigma Black Belt. Rick always loves helping a client work through a tough challenge.

Rick is an avid photographer, family history researcher, and music lover. He still practices a little chemistry in the form of wine-making and beer brewing.

Dedication

To my wife, Janet, for giving me a seat on the "happiness train", and to my sons, Ben and Andrew, for enduring some really long sports seasons, as well as for their ongoing love and support.

Acknowledgement

Thanks to Scott Carlson for editing support and general encouragement.

Introduction

It has become popular wisdom in social media circles that "If you want to succeed, then you have to fail more." While this makes a nice rhetorical argument, the pain of failure remains a powerful enough deterrent to keep most of us from following that advice. Plus, the people to whom the "fail more" message is attributed are exceptionally successful individuals like Michael Jordan, Bill Gates, Richard Branson and Steve Jobs. It's easy for them to say, "fail more" given the enormous level position of success they've achieved!

I'm not sure any of us really chooses failure in our endeavors. Some people seem to have the magic touch and succeed at everything they do. This book is not about them. Others can't seem to get a break and everything they touch goes sour. This book isn't about them either.

Instead, this story falls somewhere in between those two extremes - and it is my story. By all measures, I've had a successful professional and personal life. Still, I haven't always found life to be a bed of roses. I am aware of my failings and some of them are also known by the people who know me best. But each failure has been a turning point for me, leading to some level of triumph. Turning failures into victories is the story I want to share with you. Plus, to reward you for reading through to the end, I have some free tools to offer you to help you find success from your failures.

This book is inspired by the experience of coaching my sons through several losing seasons of recreational league baseball and football.

Like most kids, my sons wanted to play for the fun of it. But, of course, they also wanted to experience winning. There were some rough seasons for them and, as a parent, you burn through all the timeworn platitudes pretty quickly. After a while, you run out of things to say to keep your kids positive and motivated. I put that experience into some song lyrics, and I'll share those lyrics throughout the book.

We all have a capacity to manage, tolerate, or respond to failure. Some of us have a greater capacity than others. But the point is, everybody can overcome failure. What distinguishes us, perhaps, is how often we put ourselves in a position to take a risk and try something new, to achieve something we've never achieved. I know that my tolerance for this type of risk has grown. I may be more comfortable with failure than I should be, but failure doesn't frighten me the way it did when I was in my teens or twenties.

Allow me to take you on a little journey through nine of my most notable failures or setbacks. I chose these examples because they are common to many people, and because each was followed by a success.

Another truism that is oft repeated in social media circles these days is "I never lose. I either win or I learn." My stories are definitely in the "I learn" category. I hope you enjoy them, get a little laugh out of them, and find your own success stories to tell.

Table of Contents

Chapter 1

Music Career Hits a Discordant Note

"Do what you love, and you'll never work a day in your life."

I graduated in the early 1980s from St. John's University in Collegeville, Minnesota with a bachelor's degree in chemistry. I chose this major because of the great experience I had in high school taking chemistry class from Mr. Dick Slade. As a result, I got a lot of satisfaction out of my college studies as I drew closer to earning my bachelor's degree from college.

Then junior year came along.

Each of my years at St. John's I had a campus job of some sort to help me earn money to pay the bills. I washed dishes freshman year, tutored high school students in German at the adjoining St. John's Prep School during sophomore year, and worked in the Bursar's Office in my senior year. It was during my junior year, though, that I became passionate about something that distracted me from my chemistry studies - and nearly cost me my degree. I won a job as a student liturgical musician in the Campus Ministry Office.

I look back with amusement at this nearly disastrous detour: How likely was it that a chemistry major with no particular background in music would be selected to plan and perform music for the student liturgies at St. John's, the self-proclaimed center of the liturgical universe?

After all, there were plenty of St. John's music majors who were specializing in liturgical studies that would have been far more qualified than I for the liturgy planning assignment. Yet, it happened that I was chosen, and this became the first of many lessons in what it means to "follow your heart." I did have a co-planner from the music department, a superb singer named Tom.

To make the challenges of junior year in college all the more difficult, I was doubling up on my chemistry classes in order to free up time in my senior year so I could study abroad. I had two extremely difficult courses with labs to contend with, yet I was spending lots of my free time working my liturgical music job, rather than studying chemistry.

Now, keep in mind that I had scarcely performed music in front of an audience before, even though I had started playing guitar when I was about thirteen. I spent a lot of time in the recesses of St. John's Abbey with my guitar, pouring over sheet music, trying to add to my guitar skills.

All I need to say about that whole experience was that the liturgical musician job was one of the most enriching experiences I had in four years at SJU, although it left me with a conundrum upon graduation. While I just barely managed to finish my chemistry degree on time, I now decided I *really* wanted to be a liturgical musician in a church somewhere. I promptly re-enrolled in school, this time as an adult special student at the College of St. Catherine in St. Paul, affectionately known as St. Kate's. (It's a point of pride to this day that not only am I a Johnnie, but I'm also a Katie.)

Thus began my first trip down the road to career failure. I enrolled in a certificate program, not a full degree program since I didn't really have the musical chops to cut it as a full music major. However, the certification program seemed like a reasonable pathway towards my goal.

However, after one full year of taking classes, including piano lessons and music theory, it was clear I was hitting a dead end. My friends who were full music majors specializing in liturgical music weren't easily finding jobs. Further, there was no way a punk like me playing that "cowboy music" – as my Grandpa called it – was going to really make a living with just a certification in liturgical music. I dropped out of the program after the first year.

Nevertheless, out of this definite career failure came a couple of good things. I actually had the opportunity to perform as a liturgical musician at a church in White Bear Lake (the "cowboy mass" was welcome there), and I met a lifelong friend in the process, guitarist and singer John Evans.

I have since left the Catholic Church (that's a story for a different book), but I have maintained my interest in music, and I even get to play banjo once in a while with John Evans and his longtime performing partner Dan Perry. The music theory class I took remains in my Top Ten favorite classes of all time, and I've written a couple of songs of my own.

Life Lesson: Jim Collins, author of Good to Great, has written about "finding your hedgehog", in other words, that activity that balances your passion with your skills, and is something you can monetize. Liturgical music was not my hedgehog. Even if I had known that at the time, I think I still would have tried it anyway, since I'm a bit stubborn and sometimes prone to latching on to unrealistic pursuits. If you can't find your hedgehog, then reserve a place in your life for the things you are passionate about and accomplished at and let those enrich your life.

Chapter 2

A Corrosive Career in Chemistry

"Life is short... Work someplace awesome."

After coming to grips with the fact that music was not going to be my daytime vocation and dropping out of the music program at St. Kate's, I took a job with a small chemical manufacturer in St. Paul.

I chose to work for the small chemical manufacturer even though I could have accepted a position with a much larger company. While the larger manufacturer offered a more lucrative salary and greater long-term stability, I was more excited and intrigued to start my career with a small but growing company.

At first, my new job was fun and exciting because I got to work in a lab, apply the things I learned from that challenging year of double chemistry classes at St. John's and rub elbows with some pretty fun people. I accepted a pretty skimpy salary - even by 1984 standards - of $16,000 that was, however, just enough for me to buy my first car and move in to my first apartment.

What I didn't appreciate at the time was that this work environment was a bit of a set up for failure. There were some positives, of course: an interesting product, fairly unique in the industry; a huge potential market for the product and an energetic young team to promote the product.

But among the negatives of the small company: An underdeveloped technical research strategy; an enthusiastic company owner who sometimes made unrealistic promises that we in the lab couldn't support; and the straw the broke that camel's back for me… the sale of the company to a larger firm from the East Coast. The friendly little Midwestern business I initially joined now felt like a different entity once the new management team settled in.

To make matters worse, there was the stress of making the "big sale" to some large clients. I was working on a project to convince a client that our product was the right choice to protect a major bridge structure from corrosion due to exposure to the elements, and that our product would even halt any existing corrosion. Now, if you know anything about corrosion protection, you know that while it is rooted in basic electrochemistry, the field practice of corrosion protection is a bit of a black art.

My job was to conduct simulated field tests in a controlled lab environment, and show that our product could in fact meet the client's requirements, and then write the report that documented all the results. I went about conducting the testing, wrote my report, blew a little scientific smoke, and handed it over to my boss. To be honest, I don't remember anymore if that sale was completed or not.

Either way, I knew I was not going to be at the company much longer. I didn't feel that I could do my best work there.

The end came when I was up for a salary review. The company offered me a lowball raise, about $1000 (remember I was already on a puny salary). I countered by quitting on the spot. I could afford to do that since I had already moved back in with my parents by this time. The following two weeks I remember spending a lot of time moping around the house realizing that my first career stint in a corporate setting was over.

My Victory: While this experience came to a painful end, the good news is it set me on a new career choice completely. I picked up the pieces and enrolled at the University of Minnesota to earn a bachelor's degree in education. I completed my degree and earned my license in about a year and a half. Then, I began a fruitful career as a chemistry and physics teacher.

Life Lesson: Nearly 30 years after that experience, I have gained the hindsight to recognize both my failures in that situation as well as the failures of my employer. I have an appreciation for the importance of things such as onboarding of new employees, and how its leaders set the ethical values of a company. I could not have succeeded in that environment under any circumstance, and my failure was not recognizing that at the outset.

I've long since given up second-guessing my choice to take a job with the small company instead of the larger one, but I do find myself still wondering how my career path would have played out if I had taken the job with the large manufacturer. I suspect I never would have gone into teaching, a career that provided me with a lot of joy, but also with another one of my epic failures. More on that to follow.

Epilogue: Years after I left the company, I was at school where I was teaching, and received a call from the U.S. District

Attorney's office, asking me about my time working for that company. I was a little panicky, not sure if I was in trouble or not. As it turns out, the Feds were investigating the East Coast company that bought out my employer. I was working there in the years leading up to the time when the U.S. imposed trade sanctions against Libya. You may remember the days when Muammar Gaddafi was considered to be public enemy number one in this country. Just before President Ronald Reagan imposed Libyan sanctions, my company was negotiating an enormous deal with Libya to use our product to "mothball" numerous oil refineries.

The deal had not yet been signed when the sanctions were put into play. The firm that now owned my company didn't want to lose the sale, valued at seven figures. They tried to push the deal through by creating paperwork after the fact that made it look like it was a sale between Libya and their subsidiary in the

United Kingdom, thus avoiding the U.S. sanction. The punch line is that they got caught, and the two instigators of the deal were heavily fined and sentenced to serve hundreds of hours of community service in lieu of jail time. All of this activity occurred well after I had left the company. As an interesting twist, the assistant U.S. District Attorney was the parent of one of my students, so after the trial was over she was able to fill me in on some of the details, all of which is now part of the public record.

Chapter 3

A Group Lesson on Failing

"True leaders don't create followers,
they create more leaders."

Deep into my teaching career, I had switched schools from private to public, and had landed my dream position teaching honors chemistry. I inherited the role from one of my teaching heroes and mentors, who had recently retired. Over the course of my teaching career, I had always been the "junior" chemistry instructor, and hadn't ever had the privilege of teaching the honors-level course. I got my chance in 1994.

In my short time as a teacher (14 years, which by current standards is considered a long time), I worked with two of the best mentor teachers ever. First, there was Jane Tiers, a veteran teacher at St. Paul Academy and

Summit School. You had to experience Jane to fully appreciate her. She was part hobbit, part Jedi master. If you think of Linda Hunt's character Hetty on the popular CSI: Los Angeles show, you'll have a pretty good picture of what Jane was like.

My other mentor was Hank Ryan, a powerful and charismatic figure at Mounds View High School in Arden Hills, Minnesota. Legions of students have wild stories to tell about their time in Mr. Ryan's class, and most of the stories are true! Hank's claim to fame was appearing in a Pepsi commercial shot in Minnesota back in the 1970s. He happily showed that video clip to his students throughout his career.

I inherited Hank's teaching assignment around 1999. Since I knew I couldn't pretend to be like Hank, I tried to put my own spin on the class while still maintaining a high expectation of the students, as he had done.

By this time, I had 12 years of teaching under my belt so I wasn't a rookie. Still, every time you take a new assignment there's always something to learn and an adjustment period. This case was no exception.

There's always some anxiety for teacher and students alike when test time rolls around. A few weeks into the new school year and we were ready for the first unit test. All students take a while to get back into the groove after summer break, so I wasn't going to pound them too hard on our first test. Also, I was still getting to know them and their abilities. The first test came and went without a hitch.

The second unit test was a different story. This test was harder than the first, and some of the students were caught off guard. For many, it was the first time in their lives they had ever earned anything below a B, and there were more than a few students in tears. Still, we worked through it. Everybody seemed to get back on track fairly quickly and we marched on together through the first semester.

The real failure for all of us happened at the first semester final exam. This was a comprehensive final covering everything from the beginning of the semester forward. The time allotted was two hours, and I wanted the experience to be a real measure of their abilities.

Now, I had an unusual policy compared to most of my teaching colleagues, in that my tests were open note and open book. To be honest, that was a bit of a trap, because students were often lulled into a false sense of security, thinking that they didn't have to study or prepare because they could always open the book or flip through their notes. The reality was if you couldn't complete the problems without the book, you probably couldn't solve them using the book either.

Sure enough, when I gave the students their exam scores, we all had to face a bitter reality. More than 50 percent of all the honors chemistry students failed the semester exam. Wow, that was an epic failure!! Now, some teachers will make sure that an episode like this never happens by writing tests that virtually every student can pass. This way, the teacher avoids scrutiny. I, of course, opened myself up to all sorts of scrutiny and criticism, which is precisely what I got.

I spent the better part of a month dealing with upset students and the parents who love them. Again, most of these students had never experienced a setback like this in their life, so it was unfamiliar territory. Worse, the parent had never experienced it either, and so many of them went on the offensive in protection of their children. Naturally, I was the target.

I was certainly willing to take responsibility for my failings as a teacher over the course of that semester, but there were some issues where I was rock solid. I made sure that every question on the test was based on material we explicitly covered in class. There were no tricks like, "You were supposed to read that section of the book on your own." Second, I offered partial credit on lengthy problems where students completed parts correctly but ended up with an incorrect answer.

I had one student who earned a perfect score on the exam. She was a bright girl, but not necessarily a top performer throughout the semester. I asked her in front of the class why she thought she did well. She shrugged and said simply, "I studied." She was the only vindication I had that I had done my job properly, that the test aligned with the class material, and that proper preparation would lead to success.

My darkest moment through this episode was when a parent accused me of committing academic fraud, and that she was reporting me to the principal in order to achieve satisfaction and reparation. Among the claims were that I had just cost the family thousands of dollars in lost college scholarship money since her daughter now had an A- on her record (her C- exam score dropped her just below the pure A threshold to an A-). Further, the parent reasoned, because so many students had failed, clearly I was to blame. She made all sorts of demands to rectify this situation, such as suggesting I score all the exams on a curve (I never liked "curving" test scores). But I showed her that even doing that her daughter would still have earned an A-.

I'm happy to say I had the full support of my principal, who did not concede to the demands of the parent in that case. The student remained my class for the second semester, and left nothing to chance by earning outright As for the remainder of the school year. Thank goodness we were both spared the awkwardness of another "A-"!

At the next round of parent-teacher conferences a few weeks later, things were going fine when another parent brought up the question of the dreaded first semester exam. I was prepared for the worst.

"Mr. Swanson, my son failed the first semester exam is that right?" the father asked.

"Yes sir, that's true,'" I replied.

"And half of the other students failed, too?"

"Yes, that's also true.

"My son moped around the house for several days. Now, I have to ask you, Mr. Swanson, was that a difficult test?"

"Yes, it was a difficult test."

After an awkward pause that seemed to go on for hours, the father replied, "Mr. Swanson, that was a good lesson for my son. Life is difficult sometimes, and he needs to learn how to deal with that. He will study harder next time."

Oh my gosh!! I thought the parent was going to crucify me right there. But instead he just wanted validation that his son was facing challenges like he will encounter throughout his life.

My Victory: The triumphal take-away from this experience was that I learned something about being a leader and setting high expectations for performance, both for myself and for my students. Later in my career, I would think back to that time when setting performance expectation for my project teams. My victory was to honor the legacy of excellence that I inherited from the master teachers who went before me.

Life Lesson: The importance of the failure of that first semester exam was that it taught me to trust my instincts and the need to have a bit of a tough skin when facing the criticism of others.

I taught that honors chemistry class one more year before I left teaching. But the lesson stuck with me into my future job situations. It was awful while I was in the middle of it, but it was important for me to live through that. I'm a stronger leader because of it now.

Epilogue: Here's an entry from my blog, reproduced in its entirety, about the blessing and curse of being a teacher.

From the "You never can tell" file...

I had a chance encounter this morning with a former student of mine. He approached me in the parking lot at the grocery store. He had to nudge my memory - he had changed quite a bit in fifteen years - but I remembered him. He told me he had recently completed his physics degree from Augsburg College, and was now preparing to earn his teaching licensure so he could teach physics. He said the nicest thing, namely, that being in my class he knew he wanted to study physics and teach it. It took him a while to put the pieces together, but he finished the Augsburg program close to ten years after finishing high school, and he'll finish his teaching program before long. I am honored to think I had any influence in his accomplishments.

The blessing and the curse of being a teacher is that even though you know you influence the lives of your students, you never can tell exactly which ones you reached the most, or in what ways. When a former student finds you years later and lets you know, it's a nice payoff.

If you had a teacher who influenced you, find a way to tell them this week. It makes a nice Thanksgiving gift :0)

What lessons for us as business owners can we take from this story?

What influence do we have in the lives of our customers?

Maybe it's a blessing and a curse of being a business owner that you don't always know when and how you had a positive influence in the lives of your customers. Still, just think of what it might mean for your business if you strove to have a life-shaping impact on your customers. I'm talking about something much greater than, "I delivered my product or service at the price that I quoted."

Can you in your business afford to give your customers an experience of your product or service that is life-shaping or life-changing?

Can you afford not to?

Interlude 1:

Here are the first two verses and a refrain of the song I wrote thinking about my sons' experiences playing organized sports. Think of the old Johnny Cash song, A Boy Named Sue, if you want to give the words some musical context.

0 and 9

Lyrics © 2006 Richard P Swanson

When I was a kid, just ten years old, With bat and glove I went for gold

Dreamin' of the glory that was mine.

Next thing I knew, we were 0 and 8, We made the Bad News Bears look great

Headin' towards a record of 0 and 9.

REFRAIN

0 and 9, 0 and 9, Gotta win just one of these times

I'm comin' to the end of the line.

I cannot catch a lucky break,   Oh tell me just what will it take

To break this losing streak, I'm 0 and 9.

Dad said, "Son, it's part of the game.   I know that it's a cryin' shame,

Playin' hard, comin' up short, all the time."

 "You're buildin' character," was all he'd say, "Maybe you'll win another day,

For now you'll have to live with 0 and 9."

REFRAIN

0 and 9, 0 and 9, Gotta win just one of these times

I'm comin' to the end of the line.

I cannot catch a lucky break,   Oh tell me just what will it take

To break this losing streak, I'm 0 and 9.

Chapter 4

Landing in The Rough with a Franchise Business

"Stop being afraid of what could go wrong, and start being positive about what could go right."

I'm going to jump ahead in time to 2012, when I entered into a business deal that proved to be my most costly mistake, one from which I am still trying to recover two years later.

I mentioned earlier that I'm a stubborn person and even when presented with rational evidence against taking a certain action, I may go against the rational advice and proceed anyway if I am emotionally committed to it. This story is just such a case.

I was working for the Valspar Corporation in a prominent dual role as training manager and

Six Sigma black belt. I'll tell you more about that experience in an upcoming chapter. Even though I had accomplished a lot for this company and had a good reputation there, I was looking for my next challenge, and I didn't see it at Valspar. I got itchy, and started looking for something else.

I took some vacation time from work and flew myself out to Portland, Oregon to attend a three-day business workshop for entrepreneurs and business owners. Arguably I was there under false pretenses because I was neither an entrepreneur nor a small business owner. Nevertheless, the workshop presenters were nice about it and let me play along. I had an idea for a business I wanted to start, so I was able to use that model during the workshop exercises and discussions.

I arrived as the only attendee who wasn't from the Portland area. Excluding the presenters, I was the only man in a group of 16 women… sweet!

The workshop was a rapid-fire presentation of business, sales, and marketing lessons. These were things that I couldn't learn in a college classroom, I was told, but were lessons from the life experiences of the presenters.

Most of the workshop content seemed like common sense, even if it was new to me. I fit into the group just fine, again posing as a business owner, and talking about my company concept as if it were a real entity.

I left the workshop energized by the experience. The other attendees were real people who had real businesses, and I felt like I belonged in their world. They were people I could hang out with. Once I got back home, I knew I would look to connect with similar business owners and entrepreneurs for friendship and support.

A few months later two important things happened. First, I decided to leave my job to start my own consulting business. I didn't really know how and when, but I knew I was going to do it. I had latched on emotionally to the idea, and in my stubbornness I wasn't going to let go. I began putting the pieces together to insure I could cover myself financially. Somewhat against the counsel of my financial advisor and a banker friend, I planned to self fund my business and support myself using part of my accumulated retirement monies.

Although my plan was fraught with risks, I moved ahead with it in spite of the advice of people around me, and without the support of my wife, Janet. To complicate matters, Janet had just left her long time LPN position to take an hourly job at half her current wage. It was her opportunity to work normal Monday through Friday hours. We were facing the reality of living through the rest of 2012 and into 2013 on much less income than had been become our standard.

The second thing that happened was I got a call from the workshop presenters in Portland. They invited me to consider being one of the first people to own and operate a new franchise business they were launching. Their concept was to blend golf and business into a membership organization for business owners and sales leaders. They had a positive impression of me from the three-day workshop, and they thought I'd be a great candidate to be a franchisee. More than that, the franchise financial model was enticing. Projected income of $2000 per month, with growth up to $8000 per month.

I was primed and all ears for this kind of news. I was already in a risk-taking mode. "I'm already starting up one new business, why not start two?" I thought. If I get to play more golf as a result, all the better!

The franchisors sweetened the pot for me: They proposed a model of franchise ownership where I could buy exclusive franchise rights for an entire region of the Twin Cities, including four individual franchise units for the price of one. I was in, hook, line, and sinker.

I liquidated a big chunk of my retirement savings to buy my franchise area rights, on the franchise owners' promise that I would earn it all back and much more over the next 10 years. Janet was skeptical, and I did more than a little harm to our relationship by ignoring her sensibilities and moving ahead with things. She was more than gracious and charitable about it, when she didn't have to be.

The rest of 2012 and all of 2013 I spent working to get this franchise business off the ground. Given the theme of this book, you can guess how this venture turned out. During the 18 months I worked to get those first four franchise units up and running, I should have had plenty of warning that this deal was not going to pan out. I could now fill another entire book with hard lessons I learned about entering into a franchise experience.

By January of 2014, I finally realized that I had made a costly mistake with the franchise investment. The promises of the franchisors were not coming through, and I couldn't support the franchise and my consulting business any more. I cut the rope with the franchise company, forfeited my entire franchise investment (some $30,000… nothing to sneeze at!), and devoted myself entirely to my consulting business.

This was a tough pill for me to swallow. I spoke so energetically and passionately about the franchise concept, and even had one unit running at a local golf course for a short time. But after 18 months, I didn't believe the words coming out of my own mouth anymore when I spoke to people about it. If I didn't believe it, then nobody else was going to believe it, either.

I knew I deserved a big fat "I told you so!" from Janet, and it took us a while to work through the pain of the whole experience. Going forward, I have vowed to involve Janet in my decisions related to business or other major life events.

My Victory: Even though Janet never had confidence in the franchise concept, we used the experience to create a new way for us to build and deepen our own relationship: We started playing golf together.

Now it's possible that the two worst activities a married couple can do together are hanging wallpaper and playing golf. Janet and I have never tried hanging wallpaper together, but we did find a way to enjoy golf. I have spent a lot of money on clubs and lessons and league memberships trying to improve my golf game. No matter what, I'm pretty well stuck as a 24 handicapper. Meanwhile, Janet is an absolute beginner at golf. On the surface, we should have a miserable time if we go out and try to play golf together.

However, an interesting lesson from the golf franchise experience was that it's OK to bend the rules of golf a bit in order to strengthen your relationship with your golf partner. I'm not talking about cheating. On the contrary, honesty remains integral to the game the way

Janet and I play it. Rather, we don't play for score or for purpose of generating a handicap index. We play to build trust, and to grow our relationship, not to challenge it.

Life Lesson: I would like to give franchise ownership another shot some day. But I'll do my research more carefully next time, and make sure Janet is on board with the idea.

I will also follow my attorney's advice more carefully next time - he warned me of the risk, believe me! I also believe it is possible for husbands and wives to work together in a family-owned business. I've come to know numerous couples who have succeeded at this. I admire them for what they have accomplished, and Janet and I have even talked about owning a small business together some day. That chapter remains to be written.

Epilogue: After leaving the franchise company, I dropped out of touch with my other colleagues in the U.S. who had made similar deals with the franchisor. One of them reached out to me months later, to see how I was doing. We had become friends, but he found my sudden disappearance from the company unusual, and wanted to hear directly from me what had happened. We had a good chat, and I learned that a number of my other colleagues also struggled with their franchises and have since dropped out of the business, or at least have taken regular work in the mean time. I guess I wasn't the only one to have a hard time making this particular franchise concept work.

Chapter 5

The Loose Bonds of Holy Matrimony

"Everybody has a plan until they get punched in the face." - Mike Tyson

This is the hardest chapter for me to write. I had put a lot of energy into my identity as a married person and as a good husband. As you'll see, I severely damaged that image.

In many ways, I'm a late bloomer. I didn't really date anyone until after college, and I was 28 years old before I got married. I wasn't sure I'd find a life partner before I turned 30, to be honest.

But I met my future wife Lisa in 1987, when she was a dating Dan, a college buddy of mine. Fast forward a few months, and she stop dating him to go out with me. Wow, that never happened to me before!

Given my scientific mind, I assessed my relationship with Lisa in a very analytical manner. I thought our relationship met all the criteria to be a winner. We were nearly the same age, both college educated, both Catholic (that still meant something to me at the time), both teachers, both enjoyed and performed music. On paper, I thought we were destined for marital bliss.

Fast forward. Lisa and I got married, in 1989; then started our family in 1992, when Ben was born. Andrew was born in 1994.

Lisa and I were barely six months into our marriage when our communication had deteriorated to the point that we both agreed to start marriage counseling. We remained in counseling nearly uninterrupted for ten years, which in hindsight was an awfully long time. Even after all those counseling sessions, I felt more and more that I would never find the happiness I hoped for in my marriage.

We were distracted from addressing our marital trouble in 2004 when we were hit with devastating, unthinkable news. After a summer-long ordeal of doctor visits and physical examinations, our son Andrew was diagnosed with a cancerous brain tumor.

Andrew had been fighting episodes of nausea for months. He got sick on his birthday that year, and again when we surprised the boys with a Disney vacation in June. Poor Andrew spent virtually that entire vacation in our resort room with unstoppable nausea and vomiting.

On October 4, 2004 – a day I still refer to as Black Monday – Andrew had an MRI exam that revealed the tumor that was causing his sickness.

Guiding Andrew through his battle against cancer became our only focus. Although Lisa and I were united in this battle, we did not come closer together in our marriage. And once Andrew was declared cancer free in August of 2005, we were both so emotionally exhausted that I don't think we had anything left to give to each other.

My darkest days were still ahead of me, even after going through the nightmare of Andrew's cancer battle. I went down the road of marital infidelity, and started looking for a relationship with another woman.

The advent of the Internet and online dating services made this far too easy. I invented some sort of distorted rationalization about why I was justified in doing this, but I was only fooling myself. Even though I managed to keep the affair a secret for a few months, I knew I would get caught eventually. While out walking our dog Sam one day, I came clean and told Lisa what I had done.

We spent two sessions with a counselor to see if we could patch things back together. The counselor was pretty astute, and he asked me point blank if I wanted to work at restoring the marriage. I paused because I was afraid to give the honest answer. But ultimately I felt I could never be happy in the marriage, and I said, "No."

After 17 years of being married to Lisa, I filed for divorce in 2007. Our split was messy and acrimonious. I took a financial beating, and didn't see my boys for weeks once I moved out of the house. Those were the darkest days of my life. It took me a long time to re-build my relationship with Ben and Andrew, but now I have a relationship with each of my sons that is rewarding and gratifying. I'm proud of them for the young men they have become.

As for Lisa, my relationship with her is tenuous and nearly nonexistent. We do not communicate about anything anymore. That might be best at this point.

My Victory: Relationships that start as extramarital affairs aren't supposed to last. It's hard for your friends and family to put much stock in a relationship that begins under such dubious circumstances. Yet, it's been about eight years since I met Janet online.

We've been together since 2006, and I asked her to marry me in 2009. Knowing Janet has restored my confidence that I am capable of being a loving and faithful husband. As I suggested earlier, I've certainly challenged our relationship with some of my recent business failings. But Janet has shown me what happiness looks and feels like. And as I like to say, I have a seat on the "Happiness Train" thanks to her.

Life Lesson: Personal relationships live and die, business relationships live and die. I accept that now. I won't allow future relationships – especially business dealings – to go on past their time for the sake of keeping up appearances.

Chapter 6

No "Doctor" in This House

"Clinging to an old dream is like trying to get a good grip on waxed dental floss."

For the better part of my adult life I suffered from PSS – Professional Student Syndrome.

I had a fixation with college studies, and apparently four years at St. John's weren't enough. A quick survey of all the colleges and universities where I've taken classes includes: St. John's University, the College of St. Benedict, Universität Salzburg (Austria), Lakewood Community College (now Century College), College of St. Catherine's, and the University of Minnesota (three times).

I was enrolled in college classes nearly continuously from 1979 through 2006. I completed two undergraduate degrees and two graduate degrees in that time, so I guess that's pretty good. My final degree is a reminder of one of my failures in life, namely, my failure to complete my Ph.D.

I enrolled in the Ph.D. program in History of Science and Technology at the University of Minnesota in 1998. My interest in the subject dated back to my days at SJU when I took a sophomore honors course in the history of physics with Dr. Frank Rioux and Dr. Clayton Gearhart. I maintained an interest in the history of science, and especially the history of chemistry, throughout my teaching career.

While I was teaching at St. Paul Academy and Summit School in St. Paul, Minnesota in the early 1990s, I developed a unit on the subject of phlogiston, a long-since abandoned principle in the history of chemistry that was considered mainstream a couple centuries ago, but had fallen victim to the so-called chemical revolution of the mid-18th century. It turns out, that the principal of phlogiston is actually readily graspable by teenage students… it fits nicely into their existing conceptual framework. So I started teaching it to them with the hidden agenda of leading them through the same discoveries and arguments that ultimately led to its demise. Thus, I would bring my students into the world of modern chemistry.

After completing my masters degree in Curriculum and Instruction in 1996 from the University of Minnesota, I got the notion that I should pursue a Ph.D. in History of Science. There was both a practical and an egotistical motivation to do so. On the practical side, I could earn more money teaching if I held a doctorate, and on the egotistical side I could be the first member of my immediate family to earn this high of a degree (although some of my cousins had already beat me to it.)

Since I was working full-time, I rode the slow boat to my doctorate, taking just one class at a time. Also, doctoral credits were really expensive, so I was glad not to shell out more money than I had to at any one time. I painstakingly plowed my way through my coursework during the next eight years.

Some obstacles arose during that time. I left teaching in 2001, so the practical motivation and reason for earning a doctorate was now gone. However, I was too far deep into the program to want to just quit. So I continued taking classes while I was working for Twin Cities Public Television (tpt).

The bigger obstacle was dealing with the distraction of Andrew's cancer battle. I don't really know how I kept things together in those months, between continually worrying about Andrew, trying to fulfill my duties at tpt and completing the last few classes I needed before taking my written and oral exams.

In fact, I barely held things together. My written and oral exams were some of my worst performances, academically speaking. I had taken university courses for almost 25 years by then, and I simply ran out of gas. My professors graciously passed me through my exams, but I knew I had disappointed them with my performance.

I stalled for a while after exams while we continued to deal with Andrew, and by 2006, I knew I didn't have it in me – emotionally, or otherwise – to try to complete my thesis. I contacted my advisor and told him I was done. I arrived at this conclusion with a mixture of sadness and relief. I was sad to have fallen short of earning my doctorate, but I was relieved to have one less thing on my "worry plate." I knew that if I ever found myself re-motivated to complete the degree, I could re-apply to graduate school in the future.

My Victory: I didn't think there was any real way to salvage this situation. I had devoted a lot of years and a ton of graduate tuition money toward this Ph. D. program. As my relationship with Lisa deteriorated, my preoccupation with my studies became another source of friction between us and something she considered one of my major faults.

Thankfully, the director of graduate studies gave me an out. Dr. Sally Kohlstedt had been a friend and an ally throughout my years in the program. Coincidentally, I had taught her son when he was enrolled in my chemistry class back at St. Paul Academy and Summit School. She informed me that rather than simply dropping out of the graduate school and leaving my unfinished degree hanging, I could exercise an option to take a "mini-Masters" degree. I had to take some of my past written work, brush it up with a little new research, then pull together a small jury of my professors and do a "defense" of those papers. Doing that would earn me a master's degree.

That gave me just the motivation I needed to pull things together and make a graceful exit from the program. In the summer of 2006, I called the jury together, presented my papers, and made my defense. With much relief, I passed the exam. I earned a second (and very expensive) master's degree and finally closed that long chapter of my life.

Life Lesson: No matter how dire your situation, there is almost always a way out. You do have to seek out the wisdom of others sometimes, but it's better to bring things to a firm conclusion than to leave loose ends dangling.

Song Interlude #2

Here are the final two verses of my song, 0 and 9.

0 and 9

Lyrics © 2006 Richard P Swanson

The lessons of life are sometimes hard, Ya gotta play your hand no matter the cards

'Specially when all you're holdin' is one of a kind.

So stand up tall, no matter what, 'Cause sometimes about all you got

Is your character, when you're goin' 0 and 9.

The years roll by, the years roll on, I'm all grown up, I got kids of my own

And they're playin' ball, and havin' quite a time.

But now I feel my old man's pain, 'cuz somehow I gotta explain

To my kids why they're goin' 0 and 9.

REFRAIN

0 and 9, 0 and 9, Gotta win just one of these times

I'm comin' to the end of the line.

I cannot catch a lucky break, Oh tell me just what will it take

To break this losing streak, I'm 0 and 9.

Chapter 7

Painting Myself into a Corner

"Resolve lingering conflicts among team members before asking them to work on a common project solution."

To date, one of my most satisfying jobs of my career has been my position at Twin Cities Public Television, tpt. I had no business working in television production, of course, but my colleagues were very welcoming to me, and I made some lifelong friends there. They supported me and my family through those dark days when Andrew was battling cancer.

Our project was called DragonflyTV, a science series for children that was syndicated across the entire PBS network. Some of DragonflyTV's producers had previously worked on the long-running series Newton's Apple, so it was very fun for me to be part of such a talented crew. The show ultimately earned a couple of Daytime Emmy awards.

As DragonflyTV came to the end of its natural lifespan, I had to figure out what I was going to do next for work. I wasn't going to go back to teaching at the high school level; my teaching license had long since expired, plus I didn't have any energy left to give to other people's children. And I didn't have a Ph.D., so teaching at the university level was all but eliminated. I needed to find a new career path.

I began researching positions in project management and corporate training and came across something that was new to me: Six Sigma. There seemed to be all sorts of buzz on the Internet about it, especially as it related to training.

In my final years at tpt I enrolled in an online training program for Six Sigma, a process improvement methodology rooted in statistical analysis and something that looked very much like the "scientific method" that I taught my students all those years in the high school classroom. I also spent a lot of time hanging out with the project management community. They had a certification called the PMP, or project management professional.

I completed my Six Sigma training, both at the green belt and black belt levels (I didn't really get what the apparent martial arts reference was all about, but okay), and also started looking in the PMP certification process.

In mid-2007, I was newly separated from my wife, going through divorce proceedings and estranged from my kids. I was also facing the end of my job on DragonflyTV. So, this was not the most happy time in my life!

However, I did have a bit of luck on my side when Valspar Corporation in Minneapolis called me in for an interview regarding a training position. I had an offer from them in August, 2007, and so I marked my return to the chemical manufacturing industry. It was 22 years since my last position with a corporate employer.

Valspar, a Twin Cities-based paint and coatings manufacturer, hired me because of my training experience and project management background (although I never completed the PMP certification), and before long I was working on Six Sigma projects, too. I led my first green belt projects to conclusion in a timely fashion, and completed a portfolio to earn my full certification. I was ready to advance to black belt projects.

One of my most satisfying experiences at Valspar was travelling internationally. I made two major trips, one to Sao Paolo, Brazil, and a combined trip to Singapore and China. I was working on training projects in both of those regions, and I expected to be challenged both by language and by cultural barriers. In fact, I came away from those experiences believing we are far more alike than different. Yes, language and customs differ, but good people are good people wherever you go, and I'll long treasure my experiences in those other countries.

My first black belt project ended up being my most challenging, and was nearly my most significant failure in my quest to achieve black belt certification. I was project manager for an effort to streamline and simplify the way Valspar managed and completed tasks related to safety and compliance. In the world of chemical manufacturing, there are many compliance requirements issued by the government in order to ensure employee and customer safety. It truly is a full-time job just managing all those tasks, and most chemical manufacturers have employees dedicated precisely for that purpose.

Regulatory compliance is a blessing and a curse. On the one hand, it scores you points with customers and investors when you show that your company cares about employee safety. It's also good business, because it is fairly easy to show that compliant operations are, in fact, lucrative ones. The curse of compliance, however, is that it takes a lot of energy to achieve and sustain compliance, and some operations leaders can mistakenly think it is a drain on company revenues to achieve it. Everyone agrees compliance is good, but not everyone wants to spend money on it.

My project was about finding a middle ground. Valspar holds compliance in high regard, so there was no question about that, but the company also wanted to be cost-efficient at maintaining compliance. I think every company seeks that balance.

The project was based out of Valspar's manufacturing operation in the Dallas-Fort Worth area, one of its flagship production sites. On my team were three plant managers, a health and safety manager and a production manager, all from that location. Because I was based out of Minneapolis, twice each month I flew to Dallas to be with the team. The rest of the time I managed the project remotely from Minneapolis.

The first few phases of the project went well. We identified the goals of the project, started analyzing obstacles to reaching those goals, and began formulating possible solutions. Then, midway through our work, the project started to unravel. The manufacturing plant was entering its busiest season, and my team didn't have time to work on their assignments or meet with me, even when I flew down to see them.

After the project languished for more than a month, I lost confidence in myself and was afraid to report to my sponsor what was happening. I returned to Minneapolis, expecting my company to pull the plug on the project. I blamed myself for letting the project get to this point and I was certain my career as a black belt was doomed.

My Victory: One of the first things I learned about project management is that it is important to build a trusting relationship with your project sponsor. Fortunately, in this case I had a very positive relationship with mine. I also had a very smart and skilled Master Black Belt as a coach. We sat down and reviewed what was happening. In fact, my sponsor was ready to pull the plug, although he later said that he didn't consider that to be my fault or a reflection on me.

Instead, my sponsor put the project on a temporary hiatus. The team members were, in fact, committed to complete the project, but as plant managers, they also gave first priority to the everyday operations of the plant, especially when it came to getting product out the door. After a few weeks, we resumed the project, finished off the design of our solution, and the new and improved compliance process was handed off to its owner. What seemed to be a likely project failure ended being a success for the company and me.

Life Lesson: In many large companies, projects are allowed to languish uncompleted more often than they should. The project manager's role is not to push a project through no matter what, but to be the eyes and ears for the project sponsor, who has the true authority to pull the plug. I didn't understand that distinction very well going in to this project, but the lesson is clear to me now.

Chapter 8

My Disconnected Network

"The real art of trust isn't earning it, but offering it."

I left Valspar on good terms in May of 2012, after nearly five years. I wanted a new challenge, one that I had never considered right for me before until now: I wanted to start my own business and be my own boss.

When you go down this road for the first time, especially if you have no experience with small business ownership, you get lots of advice from everybody who has tried it. Naturally, I was interested in hearing their successes and failures so I could learn from them and increase my chances of success on my first try.

One success strategy I heard about repeatedly was to get your trusted colleagues to refer customers to you. That seemed like common sense to me. It wasn't long before I heard about BNI (Business Networking International), a chapter-based organization specializing in business referrals.

I found a chapter close to me, visited as a guest once or twice, and was impressed by the dollar figures reported each week. Here was a small group of just 20 business owners, yet they were on track to close nearly $1 million of business from referrals they'd given each other during the past year. Boy, I decided I could hang out with people like that! The BNI mantra is "Givers Gain!" I was ready for some of that action.

It didn't take me that long to get to know all the people in my group. The BNI chapters conduct their meetings where each member gets the opportunity to give a minute-long "elevator speech" about his or her business. My pitches were a little rough at first, but I got better at sharpening my message the more I practiced.

BNI chapters do what all business owners ought to do, namely, measure our results. The BNI system collects data such as number of referrals passed, number of dollars of business you closed from those referrals, as well as the number of dollars closed by others, based on the referrals you gave them. BNI relationships are really trust relationships, and trust takes time to build, so in your orientation training for BNI you are cautioned to be patient, let the system work, get engaged, and your numbers will grow in time.

I became a valued member of my chapter. I even received the Notable Networker Award for bringing in a lot of guests at our Visitor's Day event. I faithfully attended each week, and even started visiting other chapters as a guest, giving my elevator speech there, too.

As I approached my first anniversary with BNI, I collected my statistics. Despite my diligent efforts and the relationships I had built in my BNI chapter, I hadn't closed enough business to even cover the costs of my annual membership of $600. When it was time to renew my membership, I let my friends know I'd be dropping out of the group.

My Victory: Despite the fact that the referrals I received didn't pan out and bring me any business, my participation in BNI deepened my appreciation for small business owners and entrepreneurs. In the end, we are all sales people, I guess. I came away with some lasting personal and professional relationships, and I know I can turn to those friends and colleagues when I need their help.

Life Lesson: I spent a fair amount of time reflecting on the Givers Gain credo, and summarized my thoughts in a blog, which I present to you here in its entirety:

Reflections on the Givers Gain credo

For those of us who recently ventured into the world of small business ownership, one of the first messages we hear from others is "givers gain", and we are encouraged to adopt this credo as our own. Positioning ourselves as "givers" is a great way to earn trust with potential customers and referral partners. Here are some insights into the reality behind "givers gain".

1. What To Give

Your first challenge as a newly declared "giver" is to decide what to give. Many of you first became familiar with the giver gain motto from your participation in BNI. In that case, your "give" is fairly easy to identify… you give your BNI chapter mates leads and referrals. Fairly simple to do, it doesn't cost you anything, and the promise is they'll give you leads and referrals in return. You are giving to your colleagues the trust you earned with people whose names you share.

Outside of your participation in a BNI chapter, you might find other things to give. You might give your expertise, wisdom, or insights to interested parties in the form of a workshop, a "lunch and learn" presentation, or a webinar. Here, the give is a little more costly, not necessarily in terms of hard dollars but in terms of your time and expertise. If your business is unique because of a special product or service – what I like to call your "secret sauce" – this might be an occasion for you to spill a little secret sauce, as it were, in order to generate buzz and interest in your product or service.

Restaurant or food franchise owners know that they are going to have to give away some samples of their food in order to pique the interest of customers and gain loyal fans. Now things start to get a little costly, because you're giving away the very thing that brings in revenue.

Basic lesson: Find something of value that you can afford to give that doesn't seriously damage your income early on.

2. Givers Give

While the promise of "givers gain" is that much more will be given to you in return, this is not guaranteed. The only guarantee is that givers give, and sometimes there is no return.

I learned this lesson through personal experience. I joined BNI because I saw direct evidence of what membership in a chapter could do. After a full year of participation in a vibrant chapter, I gave my colleagues referrals that resulted in more than $20,000 of closed business. I was pretty happy about that. The flip side was that I had closed $200 worth of business based on referrals given to me. The promise of "givers gain" was not fulfilled. This is not a condemnation at all of the BNI experience. Rather, it reveals a reality that is seldom discussed or glorified, namely, givers don't always gain, but givers always give.

Basic lesson: If you are going to embrace the givers gain philosophy, you are also embracing the possibility that givers simply give. The good feeling of doing something that benefits others is a reward, no doubt, but it won't keep your business afloat.

3. Strength or Weakness?

From someplace other than BNI, I was coached to "give first, in order to earn the right to ask." I embraced this concept fully, so each time I opened a new conversation with a potential client, I made sure I had a "give" in place before asking a prospect to consider buying my services. I even listed it as a core value of my business.

One of my company advisors challenged me on this point. He offered an insight that made a strong impression on me. He suggested that publicly announcing my posture of "give first in order to earn the right…" may come off as a sign of weakness, and in fact may turn potential clients away. He countered that I have the right to ask for a client's business whether or not I first give something. As a business consultant, he reminded me that I want to appear strong and confident in front of clients, not meek or unworthy of their business.

Basic Lesson: Don't confuse the strength of generosity with the weakness of appearing unworthy.

In summary, I endorse the Givers Gain credo, but I now understand that living it has more nuances than first meets the eye.

Chapter 9

Consulting with The Boss

"In life, they say, it's better to be lucky than good.
In business, you better just be good."

Earlier I told you about my experience at the business workshop and how it emboldened me to venture out on my own. The enterprise I had in mind was a consulting business that I came to call Learning Meets Quality (LMQ). Here's its story.

When I held a blended position at Valspar that was half training manager and half Six Sigma black belt, I saw an opportunity to distinguish myself in the community of independent training consultants by bringing these two experiences together into one business. I even baked the concept into the name of my company. Hence, LMQ was born in May of 2012, right as I left Valspar.

Right out of the gate, however, I faced difficult challenges. I had no customers, no products, no sales plan, and no capital. On top of that, I was six weeks away from a planned surgery that was going to keep me on my back for about a month. And, of course, my days were soon split between trying to get my newly-purchased franchise business going, as well as my consulting business.

I was quick to spend money in the early months, dipping into my retirement funds or paying on a credit card, on the promise that a few well-chosen expenditures would pay for themselves in due course.

I spent some money on personal brand development, memberships in professional associations and even in advertising. I think I joined a dozen different organizations that I thought would help promote my business. I spent a lot of my time after my surgery going out and networking, practicing telling my story and refining my "elevator speech." I really enjoyed the freedom to plan out my days and weeks as I chose.

My first paying gig was a joint effort with a training colleague, where we did a two-day workshop back at my old employer, Valspar. It was fun to show up there and bump into some of my former mates. And receiving my first paycheck as an independent consultant was pretty nice, too. A copy of that check hangs framed on my home office wall.

Most of my energy was spent on getting "exposure". I created a workshop that I offered for free – in the spirit of givers gain, of course – in order to increase my exposure. I even had the chance to partner with the Minnesota Wild hockey team putting on this workshop. I was definitely getting exposure! [Tip: I'll share more about this workshop with you at the end of the book.]

There's a difference, I quickly learned, between exposure and sales. The former does not automatically lead to the latter. Still, my concept intrigued people, so I remained confident that I had done a good job creating a sellable business concept, and that I'd soon land my first significant gig.

However, six months into my new venture, I was for the first time gripped with doubts. My closest confidants had told me to expect things to be slow for at least the first year, and maybe the first two years. I listened and nodded when they told me that, but in my mind I was thinking, "It's not going to take me that long, I'll show 'em!" I had protected myself financially with a plan to use some of my retirement savings as needed to cover our living expenses for six months with the expectation that from that point forward I would generate enough income from LMQ to cover my ongoing expenses. By January of 2013, I needed to revisit that plan.

At my first year anniversary, I needed to start taking some serious steps to shore up my finances. I was earning a few hundred dollars a month on small jobs here and there, but I had accumulated a significant level of credit card debt… approaching $30,000. The financial hole I was in just seemed to get deeper every week.

Yet, in many ways I felt I was making progress. I had at least three significant conversations going with potential clients who liked what I had to offer, and who were in need of my services. One by one, each of those big fish slipped off the line. While I had built trust with the individuals representing each of those clients, I had not positioned myself in front of ultimate decision makers. Before long, $30,000 to $40,000 of potential revenue had slipped away. Not exactly a fortune, mind you, but more than enough to show that I had a profitable concept.

I reached the end of 2013 having generated just enough earnings with some smaller clients to encourage me to hang on for a few more months. Still, I knew I was in a bit of a pickle. I had stopped using my credit cards, both personal and business, and was stuck paying the monthly minimums. I cut off all of my memberships in professional organizations. I really became ruthless in stopping all business spending. I managed somehow to avoid falling any deeper into debt. Now I had to find a way to start climbing out.

The beginning of 2014 showed some real promise. I tightened up my marketing language and elevator speech. I narrowed the focus of my target market, and I was in new discussions for some significant consulting work. Better still, I was talking to the decision makers who had the authority to say yes, and I seemed to have them on my side. All I needed to do was close one or more of these deals, and I had a shot at keeping my business alive. It's not like all my financial woes would disappear, but I'd have a success story tell, at least.

But by May of 2014, my great expectations were dashed. Two significant potential clients fell away, each for their own reasons. I had reached the second anniversary of my business, and I had little to show for it except a lot of debt, now approaching $50,000. I made the decision I had been putting off for at least a year… it was time to face facts and prepare to shut my business down.

The week following the loss of that last client was miserable for me. I wasn't necessarily aware of it, but I had already marched through the Kübler-Ross grief stages of denial, anger, and bargaining, and now was caught in a pretty severe case of depression. Now, anyone who knows me will tell you that I'm a happy-go-lucky guy, and that I always seem to be in a good mood. So for me to enter into a full five days of the blues might be normal for most of the population, but it was highly uncharacteristic for me.

The barrage of negative self-talk running through my head amazed even me. Suddenly, all of my past failings all resurfaced, many of which I've recounted in this book.

- "You really are just average, you know that?"

- "You couldn't even finish your Ph.D."

- "You've always been an underachiever. It's no wonder you always get lowball offers from employers."

- "How could you be so blind when you bought into that franchise offer?"

- "What kind of example do you think you are setting for your kids?"

- "There's not much difference between you and the average homeless guy. Get yourself a spot at the Mission."

What really concerned me was I didn't know how I was going to get those voices to stop. Before you start worrying that I was on the brink of suicide, let me be clear I didn't harbor any of *those* thoughts. Life is too interesting to go down that road.

In time, I was able to get to the fifth stage of grief, acceptance, and that helped quiet those awful voices down. I was ready to move on to my next great thing.

My Victory: One of the best things I did as I arrived at the second anniversary of LMQ was to make an accounting of the assets I had created and accumulated during the last two years. I had coached a client through this exercise, and I thought it was the right time to do it for myself. I developed six categories of assets:

- Operational (blog content; website; marketing collateral; etc.)
- Intellectual (instructional design knowledge; project management knowledge; etc.)

- Human (StrengthsFinder™ strengths; emotional intelligence, etc.)
- Products (risk tools; documentation guides; templates; etc.)
- Services (training development; project facilitation; Six Sigma; etc.)
- Hidden (chemistry; photography; proofreading and editing; etc.)

The value I discovered was that when I added it all up, I had a list of more than 100 assets in the six categories that I could count as raw material for building a business. I hadn't just frittered the last two years away. I really had created something of my own that I could be proud of. There will be a right time when I can leverage those assets into a flourishing, thriving business of my own. The point is, I created a plan, I stuck to it, and I had something to show for my efforts when I was done.

Life Lesson: I'm not the first person to start a business only to have it shut down after two years. And I'm not the first person to start two businesses simultaneously and lose them both! The statistics on business startups that fail are a little daunting. Harvard academic Shikhar Ghosh puts the rate at 75%! I entered the game fully expecting to defy the odds and end up on the success side of the equation. That's not how it turned out.

I can easily look back on the past two years and see what some of my costliest mistakes were. Hindsight is lovely that way. But you don't drive a car forward by looking in the rear view mirror. It's time to look ahead.

Do I see my life and my career as a series of unfortunate failures? No, I really don't.

I strung nine failure episodes together for the sake of this book, but it's the victories that interest me, as I hope they interest you. It's not just an exercise in cheap psychology to say, "I never lose. I either win, or I learn." If we don't learn from our failures, I think the successes become harder to find.

Chapter 10

The Journey Continues

"Persistence is stubbornness with a purpose."

You've read the stories of my nine significant setbacks, some of them outright failures. Let's summarize the victories.

1. I kept a place in my life for the things I am passionate about. Your passion doesn't have to be your career. Find a place in your life for your passion, whether or not it makes you money.

2. I navigated a crooked career path. Your career path is not a straight line. Go ahead and put a hard 90-degree turn in your career once in a while.

3. I upheld a standard of excellence in education. Honor the legacy of excellence you inherited from those who preceded you.

4. I have kept my second marriage strong, even in the face of significant business and financial stress. Your business can be a great way to build and strengthen your relationship with the one you love.

5. I did not define myself by my worst mistake. You can defy conventional wisdom and find happiness where others say it is not possible.

6. I completed a second graduate degree. Hardware is hardware. If you can't bring home the big trophy, take the little trophy. You earned it.

7. I stood up and spoke honestly about a project that was off course. Some projects don't deserve to go to completion. Others just need to be put in "time out", like an unruly toddler.

8. I created strong and lasting relationships with fellow business owners. You build relationships with individuals, not with organizations.

9. I built a business entity with more than 100 assets that I can leverage. Create a plan, stick to it, and measure your results.

Epilogue

To thank you for picking up this book and reading it, I have two free tools and one free workshop I'd like to share with you. You can find them by visiting my website. Here's what you'll discover there.

1. Business Assets Inventory Guide

In Chapter 9, I told you about the 100+ assets I was able to list for my business. I think any small business owner or nonprofit director benefits from going through this exercise. Download the guide for free. All I ask is that you go to my blog, and leave a comment about what you learned about your organization by going through the exercise.

Here's the link to the guide:

http://learningmeetsquality.com/?p=276

Here's the link to the blog where you can leave a comment:

http://learningmeetsquality.com/business-assets-inventory/

2. Success Story Writing Guide

Michael Jordan, Bill Gates, Richard Branson, Robert Kiyosaki all will tell you that they have failed many times before achieving their success. You and I may not ever become the next mega-millionaire, but we have a story to tell, too.

Write your own success story using this guide to help you. It's a free download from my website. Go through the exercise as many times as you like. I told nine stories of failure that led to victory in this book, but I could have added a dozen more chapters. You can tell your own story. Use the guide to get some ideas down on paper, and then tweet, blog, or YouTube your story for others to read and hear.

Here's the link to the guide:

http://learningmeetsquality.com/?attachment_id=279

Tell your story on my LinkedIn group, Flames of Glory.

http://goo.gl/ux7cVr

3. Strategic Philanthropy Workshop

In Chapter 9 I mentioned my free workshop. The topic is Strategic Philanthropy, a way for business owners and nonprofits to partner together in support of their local community. You can learn more about it on my website. If you are interested in the workshop, you can contact me to work out the arrangements.

http://learningmeetsquality.com/engage/

Made in the USA
Lexington, KY
12 November 2014